MW00352134

From Your Friends At **The MA**

MAY

A MONTH OF REPRODUCIBLES AT YOUR FINGERTIPS!

Grades 2–3

Project Editor:
Amy Erickson

Editor:
Darcy Brown

Writers:
Rebecca Brudwick, Stacie Stone Davis,
Allison White Haynes, Cynthia Holcomb, Nicole Iacovazzi,
Laura Mihalenko, Kimberly Taylor

Art Coordinator:
Clevell Harris

Artists:
Cathy Spangler Bruce, Pam Crane,
Teresa Davidson, Nick Greenwood,
Clevell Harris, Sheila Krill, Rob Mayworth,
Barry Slate, Donna K. Teal

Cover Artist:
Jennifer Tipton Bennett

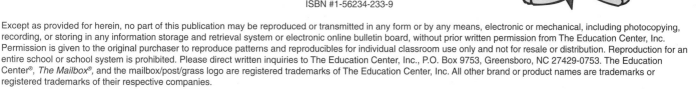

www.themailbox.com

©1998 by THE EDUCATION CENTER, INC.
All rights reserved.
ISBN #1-56234-233-9

Manufactured in the United States
10 9 8 7 6 5 4 3

Table Of Contents

May Free Time

Monday	Tuesday	Wednesday	Thursday	Friday
May 1 is May Day—a time to celebrate spring. What signs of spring have you seen? List them on a sheet of paper. 	This month is National Strawberry Month. Create and write a new recipe for a tasty strawberry dessert.	mOuse music moNey MAy List as many words as you can that begin with *m*. Then use your list to write an *m* tongue twister.	May is National Egg Month. List healthy foods that are made with eggs. 	This month is also National Hamburger Month. Ask your friends to name their favorite hamburger toppings; then make a graph to show their answers. 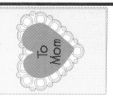
National Pet Week is the first full week in May. Write and illustrate a story about your pet or a pet that you would like to have.	A limerick is a special type of funny poetry. Edward Lear, a well-known limerick writer, was born on May 12. Read some limericks; then write one of your own.	L. Frank Baum, author of *The Wizard Of Oz* (Puffin Books, 1995), was born on May 15, 1856. In honor of his birthday, design and draw a picture of an imaginary city.	A horse named Aristides won the first Kentucky Derby on May 17, 1875. If you had a racehorse, what would you name it and why? Write your answer on a sheet of paper. 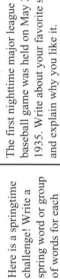	The second Sunday in May is Mother's Day. Create a card for your mother or another special woman. To Mom
May 18 is International Museum Day. If you could open your own museum, what would you have in it? Write and explain your answer on a sheet of paper. 	On May 20, 1932, Amelia Earhart became the first woman to fly alone across the Atlantic Ocean. Write about how you think she felt before, during, and after her trip.	Here is a springtime challenge! Write a spring word or group of words for each letter of the alphabet. All-Star baseball bees buzzing chicks hatching	The first nighttime major league baseball game was held on May 24, 1935. Write about your favorite sport and explain why you like it. 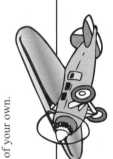	National Transportation Week is the week of the third Friday in May. Invent and draw a picture of a new way to travel. 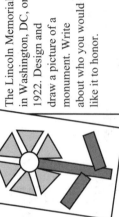
May is National Physical Fitness And Sports Month. Keep a log of each time you exercise this week. 	Go on a number hunt in your classroom! Make a list of all the places you find numbers. bus list schedule clock	Draw and color a spring picture using only triangles, rectangles, circles, and squares.	The Lincoln Memorial was dedicated in Washington, DC, on May 30, 1922. Design and draw a picture of a monument. Write about who you would like to honor.	How many different number sentences, each with an answer of 20, can you write? Be creative and show your work on a sheet of paper. $40 - 20 = 20$ $5 + 5 + 5 + 5 = 20$

Note To The Teacher: Have each student staple a copy of this page inside a file folder. Direct students to store their completed work in their folders.

May
Events And Activities For The Family

Directions: Select at least one activity below to complete as a family by the end of May.
(Challenge: See if your family can complete all three activities.)

Springtime Tale

With a touch of creativity and plenty of concentration, this oral springtime story will grow and grow! Begin the story by stating "I went for a walk in May and I saw _____." Complete this sentence with a seasonal word or words, such as "daisies blooming" or "a boy flying a kite." Then ask another family member to repeat your sentence and add another spring word or phrase. Continue the story by having each family member, in turn, repeat the entire sentence and add to it in a like manner. Put memory skills to the test by making the story as long as possible. No doubt this storytelling activity will be memorable!

Happy Birthday, Leo Lionni!

May 5 is the birthday of well-known children's author and illustrator, Leo Lionni. Many of Lionni's books teach lessons through the use of animal characters and their adventures. Read and discuss with your family some of his many books this month. If desired, invite your child to use Lionni's unique illustrations as a model to create his or her own artwork. Then have him or her write a story to accompany it.

A Color Of His Own (Alfred A. Knopf Books For Young Readers, 1997)
An Extraordinary Egg (Alfred A. Knopf Books For Young Readers, 1994)
Fish Is Fish (Alfred A. Knopf, Inc.; 1974)
It's Mine! (Random House, Inc.; 1996)
Matthew's Dream (Random House, Inc.; 1995)

National Pet Week

To promote awareness of animal care, this event is held each year during the first full week of May. Explore with your family the many types of pets and their different needs and characteristics by playing Guess My Pet. To play this variation of the popular game Twenty Questions, one player thinks of a pet without revealing it. In turn, each remaining player asks him or her a question about the pet that can be answered by either "yes" or "no." After receiving a response to the question, the player may guess the animal's identity. If the player correctly names the animal, he or she is declared the winner of this round and may think of the next mystery pet. If the guess is incorrect, play continues in a similar manner. For added fun, see who can guess each animal with the fewest number of questions.

Note To The Teacher: Distribute one copy of this reproducible to each student at the beginning of the month. Encourage each family to complete at least one activity by the end of May.

4

Cinco De Mayo

Celebrate Cinco De Mayo with these festive activities and reproducibles! This Mexican holiday is observed each year on May 5. Cinco De Mayo commemorates the historic Battle Of Puebla. During this battle, Mexican troops successfully defended their country from the invading French forces. So strap on your sombrero, put on your sarape, and head south of the border for some learning fun. Olé!

Number Words		
English	Spanish	
one	uno	(OOH-noh)
two	dos	(DOHSS)
three	tres	(TRACE)
four	cuatro	(KWAH-troh)
five	cinco	(SEEN-koh)
six	seis	(SACE)
seven	siete	(see-EH-tay)
eight	ocho	(OH-choh)
nine	nueve	(NWEY-bay)
ten	diez	(DEE-ACE)

Uno, Dos, Tres...

Students will be número uno fans of this concentration game! First teach youngsters how to count to ten in Spanish (see the reference on this page). Give each student a copy of page 7 and have him cut apart the game cards. Then assign each student a partner. To play, each student pair places one set of cards facedown. Each student in turn flips over two cards and reads aloud the Spanish words. If the student has revealed a matching numeral card and picture card, he keeps the match. If no match is made, the student turns the cards facedown again. The student with the most cards at the end of the game is the winner.

Story Sombreros

Have students put on their creative-writing hats with this thought-provoking activity! Give each student a copy of page 6 and have him read the story starters. Then instruct each youngster to write a story on his sombrero with his favorite story starter. Ask him to lightly color the sombrero as desired, being careful to leave his writing visible. Have each student cut out his sombrero; then display all of the completed projects on a brightly colored bulletin board titled "Hats Off To Cinco De Mayo."

Fiesta Fun

Culminate your study of Cinco De Mayo with this fun-filled fiesta! Help your youngsters decorate the classroom fiesta-style with piñatas and murals. Ask volunteers to bring festive Hispanic foods and invite parents and staff to attend this special event. Have your students perform a short skit or song in Spanish or a Mexican dance. After the performance, play mariachi band music and serve the refreshments. What a fun way to say adiós to your Cinco De Mayo unit!

Story Sombreros

You are having a Cinco De Mayo party. What activities will you plan for your guests?

This is a special *sombrero*—if you put it on, you will get one wish. What would you wish for if you could wear this hat?

Maria was sure that the *piñata* would break open with one more hit! She swung the stick, took off her blindfold, and could not believe what she saw. *Finish the story.*

It's Cinco De Mayo! You are going to cook a special Mexican food. Write about this food, but don't tell its name. See if a classmate can guess what it is!

Note To The Teacher: Use with "Story Sombreros" on page 5.

uno — burro	1 — uno	dos — banderas	2 — dos
tres — piñatas	3 — tres	cuatro — guitarras	4 — cuatro
cinco — sarapes	5 — cinco	seis — iguanas	6 — seis
siete — tacos	7 — siete	ocho — maracas	8 — ocho
nueve — sombreros	9 — nueve	diez — chiles	10 — diez

Note To The Teacher: Use with "Uno, Dos, Tres…" on page 5.

Celebrating Cinco De Mayo

Read the paragraph.
Use the words on the chiles to fill in the blanks.
Color each chile when you use its word.

Cinco De Mayo is one of Mexico's most important fiesta days. It honors the Mexican victory over the French at the Battle of Puebla. This happened on May 5, 1862. The French tried to take over the country, but the Mexican people stopped them. Now people in Mexico and parts of America celebrate this special event on Cinco De Mayo. They have parades, fireworks, and parties. Cinco De Mayo is a time to remember the importance of freedom.

1. Cinco De Mayo honors the Mexican _____ over the French.

2. The Mexican people fought against the _____ in the Battle of Puebla.

3. Cinco De Mayo is celebrated with parties, parades, and _____.

4. People in parts of America and in _____ celebrate Cinco De Mayo.

5. The Battle of Puebla happened on _____ 5, 1862.

6. Cinco De Mayo is an important _____ day in Mexico.

7. Cinco De Mayo is a celebration of _____.

fiesta

victory

fireworks

French

Mexico

May

freedom

Fiesta News Flash

Read Iggie's story.
Cut out each picture.
Glue each picture in the correct box.

1. ☐ are served at this fiesta.

2. ☐ is the day of the fiesta.

3. When the ☐ broke, the candy spilled out.

4. Iggie could hear the ☐ band playing.

5. Iggie ☐ is reporting live from the fiesta.

6. Each boy is wearing a ☐ on his head.

7. Each girl is wearing a ☐ in her hair.

This is Iggie **Iguana** reporting live from the **Cinco De Mayo** Fiesta. There are many foods to choose from here: fresh **tortillas,** tacos, burritos, and churros. The **mariachi** band is playing. The **piñata** was just broken. The children are racing toward the candy! Each boy is wearing a **sombrero.** Each girl has a **flor** in her hair. We're having a great time here at the fiesta. Come on over before it ends!

mariachi

sombrero

Tortillas

May 5
Cinco De Mayo

flor

piñata

Iguana

Name _____

Cinco De Mayo
Addition and subtraction:
3-digit without regrouping

Piñata Party

Solve each problem.
Use the code to color
the piñata.

Color Code:
If the answer is
• greater than 500, color
  the box green.
• less than 500, color
  the box red.

① 192
  + 302

② 372
  + 304

④ 956
  − 134

⑤ 586
  − 225

③ 715
  + 164

⑥ 692
  − 131

⑦ 662
  − 251

⑧ 246
  + 340

⑨ 312
  + 376

⑩ 608
  − 403

⑪ 293
  + 204

⑫ 874
  − 162

Bonus Box: On the
back of this sheet,
order from smallest
to greatest all of the
red-colored answers.

Frolic With Frogs

Looking for a way to leap into spring? Then "ribbet" students' attention with these fun-filled frog activities and reproducibles!

Surprise, Flies!

Students will be buzzing like flies over this fast-paced game. Label each of four large lily-pad cutouts with a different numeral from 1 to 4. Display each one in a separate area around the perimeter of your room. Then ask a student volunteer to be a frog and have the remaining children be flies. Give the frog several index cards, each of which has been programmed with a pond-related word having one, two, three, or four syllables. (For the best results, use an equal number of one-, two-, three-, and four-syllable words.) Direct the frog to stand in the center of the room with his eyes closed and have him start counting aloud to ten. As he counts, ask each fly to quickly and quietly "fly" to one of the lily-pad areas. When the frog reaches the number ten, he opens his eyes, reads a word card aloud, and identifies the number of syllables in the word. The flies in the area with the corresponding numeral are "caught" and must return to their seats. This round continues in a like manner until only one fly remains; then that fly becomes the frog for the next round.

From Tadpole To Frog

Demonstrate the life cycle of a frog with this hands-on activity! Give each student two brads and a copy of page 13. Have him color and cut out each pattern piece. Explain that he will use these pieces to show a frog's life stages. Tell students that a tadpole has a long tail. As it grows, the tadpole develops lungs and its back legs appear. Instruct each youngster to attach two back legs to the tadpole's body with a brad as shown (dark dots on the patterns indicate the correct placement). Tell students that the tadpole then develops front legs, and its tail shrinks and disappears. Have students show this stage of development by attaching front legs to their tadpoles with brads and carefully cutting off the tadpoles' tails. Have student volunteers use their paper frogs to retell the life cycle; then display each youngster's completed project on a brightly colored bulletin board throughout your study of frogs.

Terrific "Toad-als"

Jump-start students' addition skills with this unique learning center! Duplicate, color, and cut out several frogs and logs (patterns on page 12). Use a permanent marker to program each frog with a different single-digit numeral and each log with a numeral from 6 to 20. Laminate the cutouts for durability if desired. Place the cutouts in a decorated envelope or container in a center. To use the center, a child chooses a log. Then she finds three frogs with numerals that, when added together, equal the numeral on the log. Challenge students to find more than one solution for each log. Now that's a center that will have students learning by leaps and bounds!

11

Patterns

Use with "Terrific 'Toad-als' " on page 11.

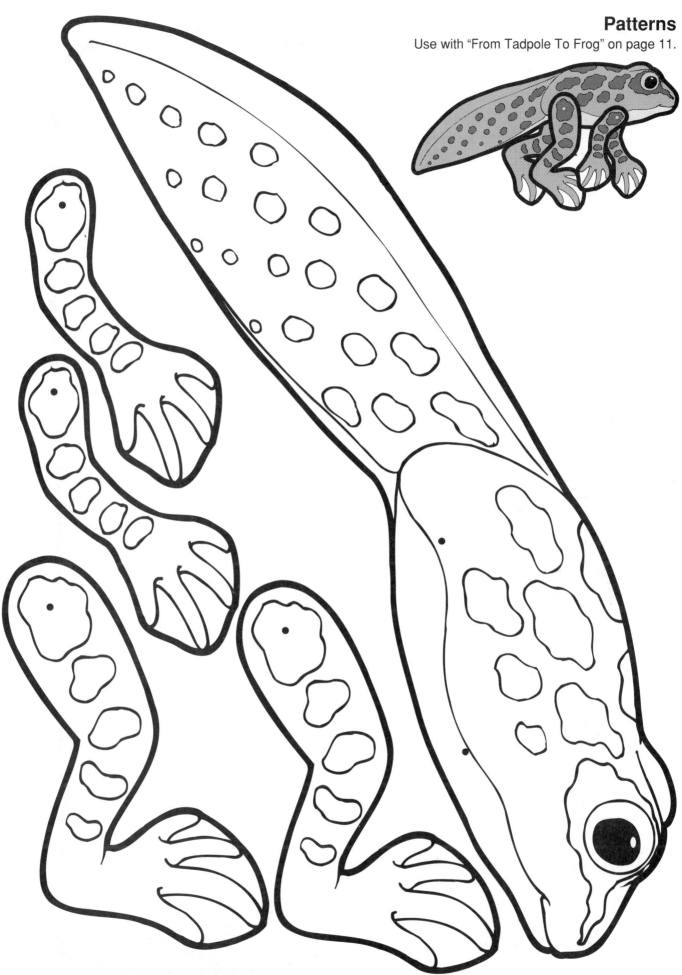

"Pond-ering" Parts Of Speech

Write a word in each box to match the letter and part of speech.
The first one has been done for you.

	f	r	o	g
noun	frog			
verb				
adjective				
adverb				

Bonus Box: Choose a noun, a verb, an adjective, and an adverb from your chart. On the back of this sheet, write a sentence with these words and illustrate it.

Name _____

"Froggy" Feast

Write the words in ABC order.
Color each fly as you use its word.

frog

leap

tadpole

spot

green

splash

fly

float

grass

friend

leg

tail

1. _____   5. _____   9. _____

2. _____   6. _____   10. _____

3. _____   7. _____   11. _____

4. _____   8. _____   12. _____

15

Patchwork Puzzle

Solve each problem.

24 + 7	46 − 8	75 + 19	62 − 14
31 − 16	87 + 5	90 − 47	12 + 38
54 + 29	83 − 16	68 + 17	77 − 18
43 − 19	35 + 35	51 − 38	24 + 38

Cut on the dotted lines.
Glue each answer to the
matching problem on the grid.

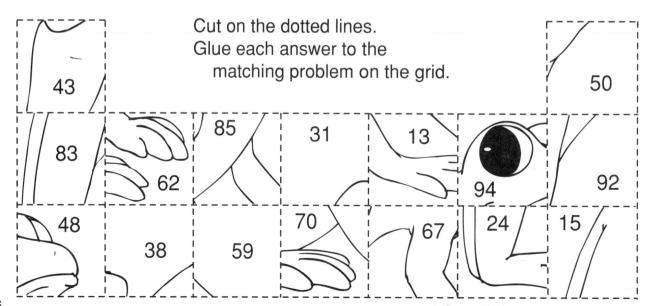

43   85   31   13   50

83   62   94   92

48   38   59   70   67   24   15

GET BUZZIN' WITH BEES

What's the buzz? Why, it's a honey of a unit that will keep your students as busy as bees!

Busy, Busy Bees

Is the buzz the most important part of a bee? Not by a long shot! We depend on bees to pollinate flowers and crops. Also, bees produce honey and beeswax. Beeswax is used to make candles, floor wax, lipstick, and furniture and shoe polishes. Crayons, waxed paper, and even chewing gum come from beeswax, too. Share this information with students; then have each student finds in discarded magazines at least five pictures showing products or contributions made by bees. Instruct him to cut out each picture, glue it onto a different precut construction-paper shape, and write a label below it. Then have the youngster hole-punch the top of each shape and tie it to a coat hanger with a length of yarn. To complete his mobile, each student draws and cuts out a construction-paper bee and tapes it to the top of his hanger. Use yarn or monofilament to suspend the completed projects from the classroom ceiling for an "un-bee-lievable" display.

How Sweet It Is!

This honey of an activity provides sweet inspiration for persuasive writing. Purchase a jar of honey and give each student a sample to taste. Then distribute a copy of pages 18 and 19 to each student. Have him "invent" a brand of honey and design a label for it on his honey jar. Next have him color and cut out his jar, then write an advertisement on page 19 to promote his brand of honey. Challenge him to include at least two facts and two opinions in his ad. Then have him glue his completed ad and honey jar to a large sheet of construction paper. Invite students to share their ads and ask their classmates to identify the facts and opinions included. What a sweet way to build writing skills!

Sweet Treats

Introduce the anatomy of a honeybee with a lesson that's truly good enough to eat! In advance, gather these ingredients: 2 cups peanut butter, 1 cup honey, 2–3 cups powdered milk, a bag of slivered almonds, and a package of black shoe-string licorice. (These ingredients will make about 48 bees.) Cut the licorice into pieces approximately 1" long. Each student will need eight licorice lengths. Have students help you combine the peanut butter, honey, and two cups of powdered milk in a medium-sized bowl. Gradually add more powdered milk until the dough is easy to handle. Give each student two rounded tablespoons of the dough on a piece of waxed paper. Instruct her to form with the dough a bee's body in three segments: a head, a thorax, and an abdomen. Next have each student press four almond slivers into the thorax for wings. Ask each youngster to insert two precut lengths of licorice into her bee's head to represent antennae and six licorice lengths into its thorax for legs. Review each of the bee's body parts with students; then invite youngsters to nibble away at their sweet treats!

17

How Sweet It Is!

Note To The Teacher: Use with "How Sweet It Is!" on page 17.

Name _____

Honey Hunt

Use the graph and key to find the number of flowers each bee visited.
Then answer each question.

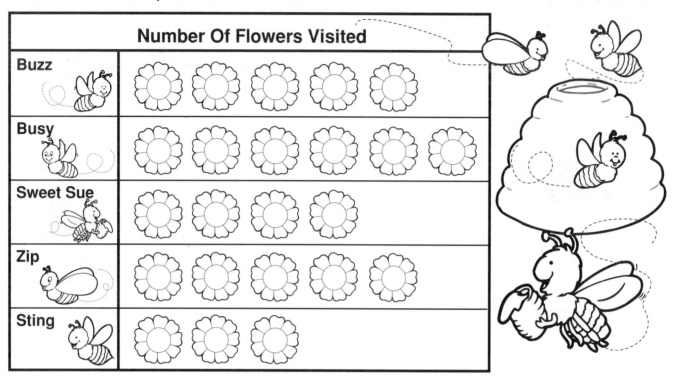

Key: ✿ = ☐ flowers

1. How many flowers were visited by Buzz? _____   Busy? _____

   Sweet Sue? _____   Zip? _____   Sting? _____

2. Who visited the greatest number of flowers? _____

3. Who visited the smallest number of flowers? _____

4. Which two bees visited the same number of flowers? _____

   _____

5. How many more flowers did Busy visit than Sting? _____

6. How many flowers did Buzz and Sweet Sue visit altogether? _____

Bonus Box: On the back of this sheet, write two sentences about this graph.

Note To The Teacher: Duplicate one copy of this page. Write a number in the box; then duplicate a class supply.

Home, Sweet Home

There are many kinds of bees and bee homes. Bees make their homes in the ground, in shells, and even in people's houses! Read about some different bees and where they live.

Leaf-cutting bees make their homes in wood, under bark, or in the ground. They line their homes with leaves.

Mason bees sometimes live in empty snail shells or under stones. Sometimes they build homes in tunnels made by other bees!

Mining bees let their queen choose a home. She makes a tunnel in the ground with waterproof rooms to protect her young.

Carpenter bees work with wood, but they don't use hammers and nails! For their homes, they dig holes in wooden porches and barns.

Honeybees build homes called *hives*. Workers called *fanner* bees beat their wings to help cool their hive.

Complete each sentence.

1. Leaf-cutting bees are found near trees because _____

   _____

2. Mason bees might look for an old bee tunnel since _____

   _____

3. The queen mining bee makes a waterproof home because _____

   _____

4. Carpenter bees make some people upset since _____

   _____

5. Fanner honeybees beat their wings because _____

   _____

Bonus Box: On the back of this sheet, write the names of these five kinds of bees in ABC order.

Homophone Hives

Choose the correct word to match each definition.
Write the word on the hive.

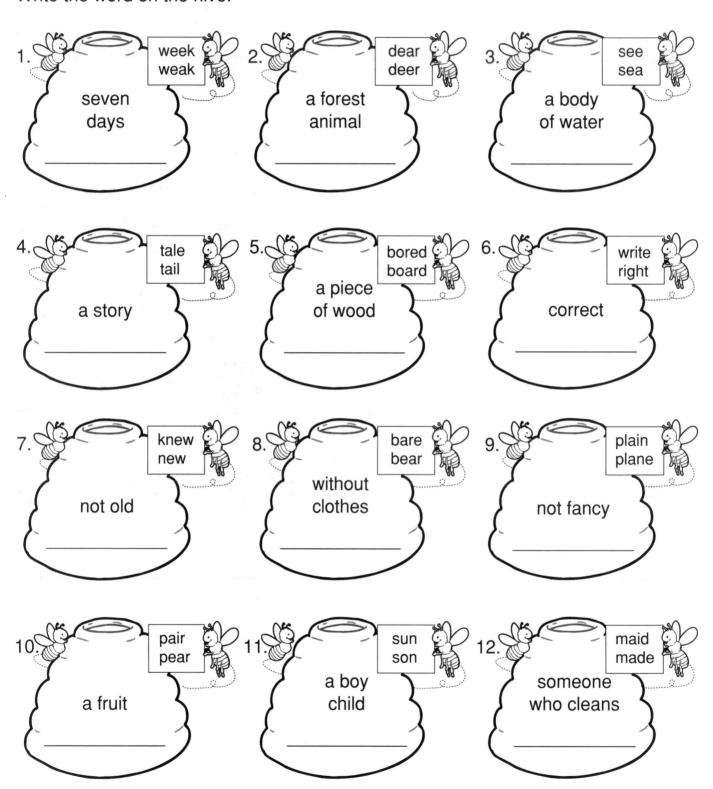

1. week / weak

seven
days

_____

2. dear / deer

a forest
animal

_____

3. see / sea

a body
of water

_____

4. tale / tail

a story

_____

5. bored / board

a piece
of wood

_____

6. write / right

correct

_____

7. knew / new

not old

_____

8. bare / bear

without
clothes

_____

9. plain / plane

not fancy

_____

10. pair / pear

a fruit

_____

11. sun / son

a boy
child

_____

12. maid / made

someone
who cleans

_____

Bonus Box: Choose five pairs of homophones. Write a sentence with each pair of words.

CALLING ALL COWPOKES!

Gallop into a rodeo of Wild West activities with your young buckaroos!

Rodeo Review

Rodeos began as small contests between cowboys. Once or twice a year, the cowboys would round up the cattle and take them to market. When the cowboys were paid for their work, they celebrated by holding competitions to show off their skills.

Review addition, subtraction, and vocabulary skills with a classroom rodeo. In advance, duplicate and cut out a class supply of the patterns on page 24. Program each boot with an addition problem, each hat with a subtraction problem, and each horseshoe card with a vocabulary word. One set of cards will be used for each round, or rodeo event. Divide students into small teams and have each team stand in a line. Present a problem or word from one set of cards to the first person on one team. He solves the problem or uses the word in a sentence, then moves to the end of his team's line. His team earns one point if he has answered correctly. If he has answered incorrectly, the same card is presented to the next team. Play continues in this manner with the remaining cards in the set. Additional rounds are then played with the remaining sets of cards. Present stickers or other small prizes to the team with the greatest number of points.

Research Roundup

Have your students explore the Wild West by rounding up facts! Gather a supply of reference materials in advance. Duplicate a class supply of page 25 and program each sheet with a question about cowboys or their work. (Refer to the sample questions shown.) Give each student a programmed sheet and ask him to complete it using the reference materials provided. Then have each youngster share his information with the class.

What kinds of food were carried in a chuck wagon?

What kind of clothes did a cowboy wear?

What are some things that happened during a roundup?

What are some different breeds of horses?

Lasso The Lingo

bronco—an untamed horse

chaps—leather coverings to keep thorns and branches from tearing trousers

chuck wagon—a wagon that carries food, utensils, and bedding

corral—an enclosed yard

lariat—a rope

quirt—a small whip for controlling a horse

roundup—a gathering of horses for a total count

rustler—a cattle thief

tenderfoot—a person new to being a cowboy

wranglers—cowboys who look after the horses on a ranch

Patterns

Use with "Rodeo Review" on page 23.

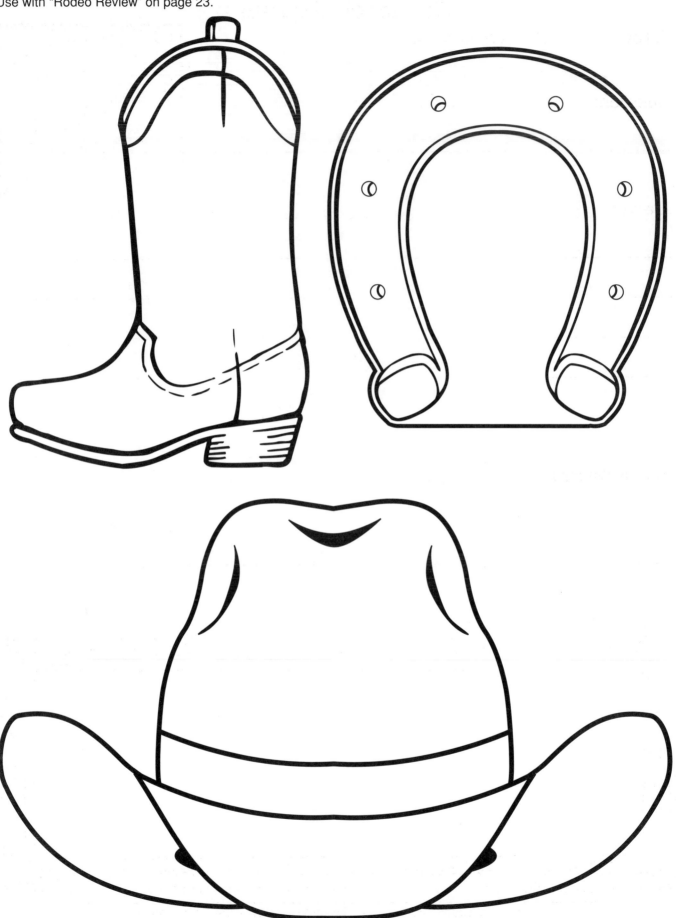

Name _____

Research Roundup

Follow your teacher's directions.

Question: _____

_____

Answer: _____

_____

_____

_____

_____

_____

Here is where I found my answer: _____

_____

_____

This is a picture about what I learned:

Bonus Box: On the back of this sheet, write two more facts about cowboys and their work.

©1998 The Education Center, Inc. • *May Monthly Reproducibles* • Grades 2–3 • TEC953

Note To The Teacher: Use with "Research Roundup" on page 23.

Cowboy Chili

Slim is in charge of making chili for the hungry cowboys in the bunkhouse.
He has the chili recipe, but he has mixed up the steps for making it.
Help Slim by cutting out the steps and gluing them in the correct order.

Cowboy Chili
3 pounds ground beef
2 medium onions, cut into small pieces
2 cans (26 ounces each) kidney beans
2 cans (16 ounces each) stewed tomatoes
1 can (46 ounces) V8® vegetable juice
chili powder (optional)

Step 1:
Step 2:
Step 3:
Step 4:
Step 5:

Add the rest of the ingredients to the cooked meat and onions.

After the meat and onions are cooked, drain the fat.

Stir all of the ingredients together; then cook the mixture for one hour.

Cook the ground beef and onions together.

Serve the chili to a heap of hungry cowboys.

Note To The Teacher: One recipe of "Cowboy Chili" serves a class of 30 students.

Hats Off!

Read the paragraphs.

A cowboy's hat was an important part of his outfit. The shape of the hat was special. The deep crown of the hat kept it on the cowboy's head when he was riding a horse. The hat's wide brim kept sun and rain off his face.

The cowboy's hat helped him with his work, too. He could wave his hat to make a herd of cattle move. He could also use it to signal another cowboy in the distance.

The hat had other uses, too. When he was thirsty, a cowboy could scoop water from a stream with it. At night, the cowboy could place the hat under his head for a pillow. A cowboy really depended on his hat!

Imagine that you are a cowboy hat.
Use the information on this page to write about your day.

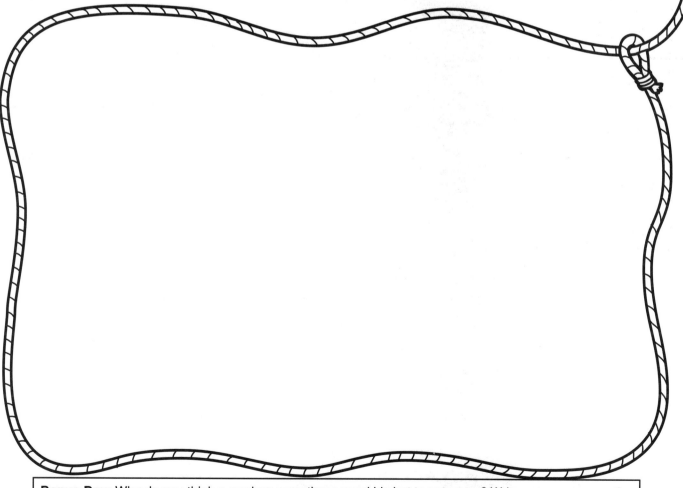

Bonus Box: Why do you think a cowboy sometimes used his hat to get water? Write your answer on the back of this sheet.

Kick Up Your Heels!

Read each problem carefully.
Underline the word or words that help you decide to add or subtract.
Solve the problem in the boot.

1. Cowboy Carl rounded up 46 cows. Tough Tex rounded up 27 more. How many cows were rounded up in all?

2. Chuck-Wagon Charlie made 78 biscuits. He served 29 of them. How many biscuits were left?

3. Lasso Lilly bought 34 horses for her ranch. She already had 36 horses. How many horses did she have altogether?

4. Bronco Bill sold 83 rodeo tickets. Brother Bud sold 65 tickets. How many more tickets did Bronco Bill sell?

5. Tumbleweed Tess had 42 bales of hay. She used 26 bales to feed her cattle. How many bales did she have left?

6. Dakota Dan trained 17 wild mustangs. He also trained 14 stubborn mules. How many animals did he train altogether?

7. Bowlegged Bob roped 32 ponies. Sagebrush Sue roped 27 ponies. How many more ponies did Bowlegged Bob rope?

8. Slim saw 51 coyotes howling at the moon. Then 45 of them fell asleep. How many coyotes were left howling?

9. Dusty counted 35 jackrabbits on the prairie. Rusty counted 16 more jackrabbits. How many jackrabbits were there in all?

10. Thunder Hoof threw 19 riders. Later he threw 23 more. How many riders did he throw in all?

Bonus Box: On the back of this sheet, write your own word problem. Ask a classmate to solve it.

UNDER THE SEA

Dive into this collection of seafaring, skill-boosting activities!

In The Deep Blue Sea

Capture student interest and enhance your study of the ocean with this informative bulletin board. Cover a bulletin board with blue background paper and staple construction-paper seaweed to the bottom of the display. Instruct each student to write on a large construction-paper fish a question she would like to have answered during the ocean study. Have the youngster sign her name; then use a pushpin to display each fish on the bulletin board. As a question is answered during your ocean study, remove the corresponding fish and return it to the student who wrote the question. Have her write the answer in a complete sentence on the back of the fish. Then reattach it to the display with a pushpin so that the answer is showing. By the time your study is completed, your class will have quite a catch of fishy facts!

Creatures Of The Deep

Take a look at some unusual creatures of the deep with these student-made booklets. Duplicate pages 30–32 for each student and give him a copy of each page. Read and discuss the facts with students. Then have each child cut out and glue each fact strip under the corresponding animal on his booklet pages. Ask him to color and cut out the pages and glue his pages together at the tabs. Then help each student accordion-fold his completed pages as shown. Have each youngster partially unfold his booklet so that it is self-standing, and display these informative ocean scenes for all to see.

Booklet Cover
Use with "Creatures Of The Deep" on page 29.

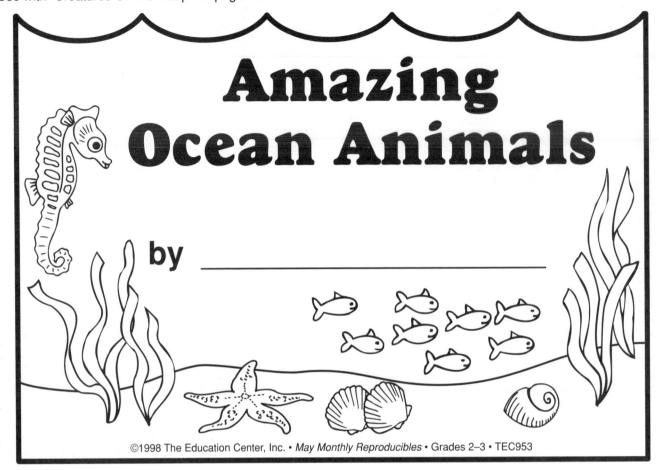

Amazing Ocean Animals

by _____

Fact Strips
Use with "Creatures Of The Deep" on page 29.

The **Pacific leatherback turtle** can grow to seven feet long. It can weigh 1,000 pounds. This animal is the largest reptile in the sea.

The tiny **blue-ringed octopus** is only about one inch long. Even so, it is one of the most poisonous creatures in the world.

The **deep-sea anglerfish** looks like it has a fishing pole on its head. This "pole" has a light on the end that hangs by the fish's mouth. The light attracts prey.

The **garden eel** lives with its tail buried in the sand. This eel uses its mouth to grab food that floats by.

The **flying fish** has fins that look like wings. It can leap five feet above the surface of the water.

The **gulper eel's** jaws open wide to scoop up fish larger than itself. The gulper eel has a lighted tail to attract prey.

The **tiger shark** catches prey with its teeth. It has several sets of teeth. When some fall out, more teeth move forward.

The **sea dragon** is a relative of the sea horse. It has flaps of skin that look like seaweed.

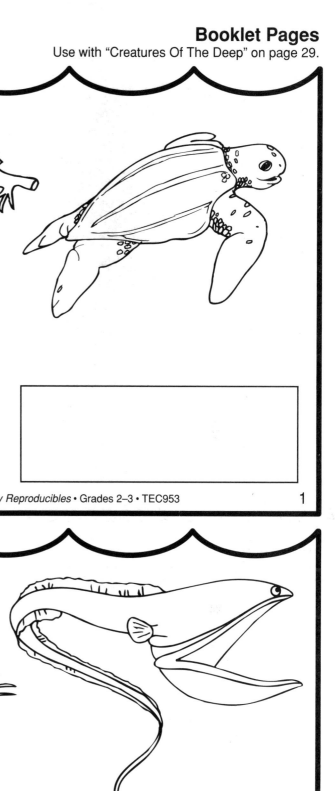

Glue to the right edge of the cover.

©1998 The Education Center, Inc. • *May Monthly Reproducibles* • Grades 2–3 • TEC953

1

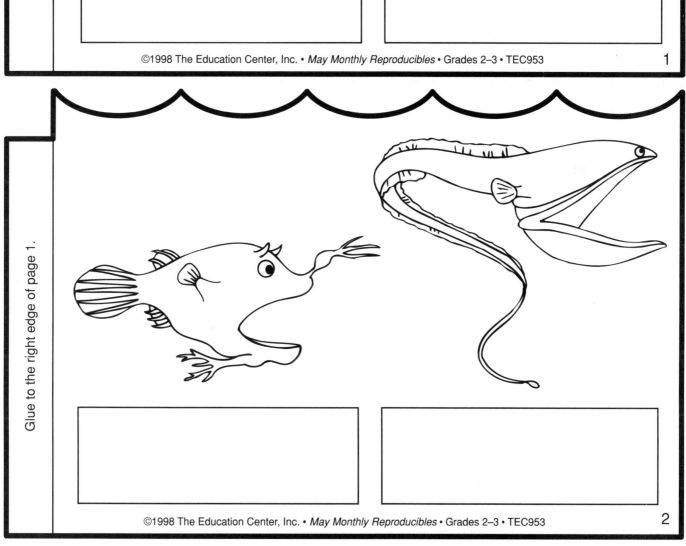

Glue to the right edge of page 1.

©1998 The Education Center, Inc. • *May Monthly Reproducibles* • Grades 2–3 • TEC953

2

Booklet Pages

Use with "Creatures Of The Deep" on page 29.

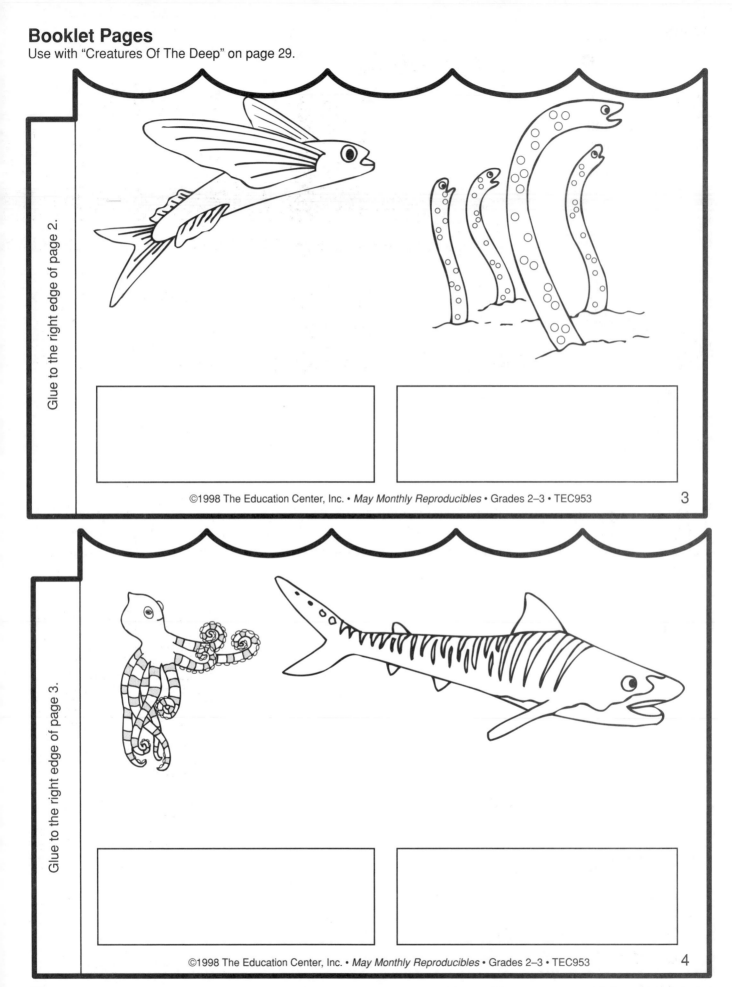

Glue to the right edge of page 2.

©1998 The Education Center, Inc. • *May Monthly Reproducibles* • Grades 2–3 • TEC953

3

Glue to the right edge of page 3.

©1998 The Education Center, Inc. • *May Monthly Reproducibles* • Grades 2–3 • TEC953

4

Name _____

Seaside Synonyms

Words with the same meaning are called **synonyms**.
Cut out each shell card.
Read the words on each shell.
If the words have the same meaning, glue the shell card
   onto the pail.

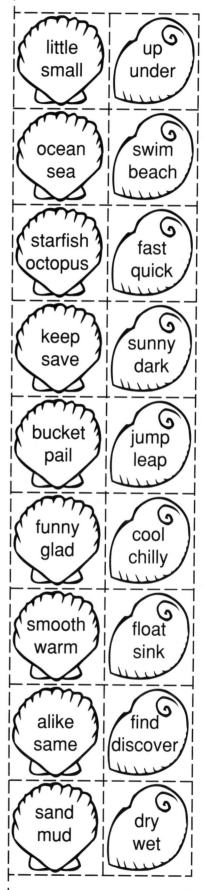

little small	up under
ocean sea	swim beach
starfish octopus	fast quick
keep save	sunny dark
bucket pail	jump leap
funny glad	cool chilly
smooth warm	float sink
alike same	find discover
sand mud	dry wet

Bookmarks

*The Magic School Bus On
The Ocean Floor*
by Joanna Cole
(Scholastic Inc., 1994)

What Do You See Under The Sea?
by Bobbie Kalman
(Crabtree Publishing Company, 1995)

An Octopus Is Amazing
by Patricia Lauber
(HarperCollins Children's Books, 1996)

Seven Seas Of Billy's Bathtub
by Ray Nelson, Jr. & Douglas Kelly
(Flying Rhinoceros, Inc.; 1997)

The Ocean Alphabet Book
by Jerry Pallotta
(Charlesbridge Publishing, Inc.; 1989)

Rainbow Fish To The Rescue!
by Marcus Pfister
(North-South Books Inc., 1995)

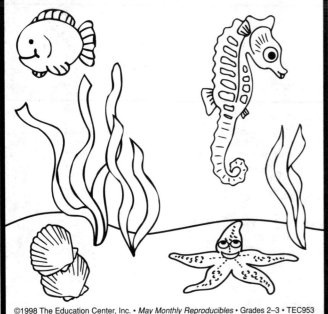

*The Magic School Bus On
The Ocean Floor*
by Joanna Cole
(Scholastic Inc., 1994)

What Do You See Under The Sea?
by Bobbie Kalman
(Crabtree Publishing Company, 1995)

An Octopus Is Amazing
by Patricia Lauber
(HarperCollins Children's Books, 1996)

Seven Seas Of Billy's Bathtub
by Ray Nelson, Jr. & Douglas Kelly
(Flying Rhinoceros, Inc.; 1997)

The Ocean Alphabet Book
by Jerry Pallotta
(Charlesbridge Publishing, Inc.; 1989)

Rainbow Fish To The Rescue!
by Marcus Pfister
(North-South Books Inc., 1995)

Note To The Teacher: Duplicate and cut out a bookmark for each student. Send it home with the youngster and encourage him to read the listed books.

Memorial Day

Wrap up May with a patriotic tribute to Memorial Day!

Holiday Facts

- Memorial Day honors Americans who have fought and died for our country.
- Most states observe Memorial Day on the last Monday in May.
- Memorial Day is sometimes called *Poppy Day* because volunteers sell red poppies to help disabled veterans.
- Memorial Day is also known as *Decoration Day*. Flowers and flags are often placed on the graves of military personnel and loved ones.
- Special patriotic programs and parades are held on this day.

Tribute Triaramas

Reinforce the meaning and traditions of Memorial Day with this unique 3-D project! Share with youngsters the background information provided on this page. If desired, also read aloud and discuss a book about this holiday, such as *Memorial Day* by Lynda Sorensen (The Rourke Press, Inc.; 1994). Use the instructions shown to have each student make a triarama that illustrates what he has learned about this holiday.

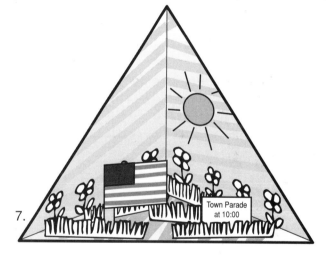

7.

Making A Memorial Day Triarama

Materials:

one 12" white construction-paper square
colorful construction-paper scraps
crayons
scissors
glue

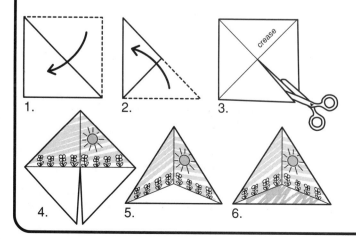

Directions:

1. Fold the construction-paper square in half diagonally (from one corner to the opposite corner).
2. Fold the paper in half again.
3. Unfold the paper and cut along one fold line to the center of the square.
4. Position the square in front of you with a point at the top and the cut at the bottom (see illustration). Color a Memorial Day scene or things related to this holiday on the top half of the paper.
5. Overlap the two bottom triangles until their corners meet and glue them in place.
6. Color the bottom of the resulting triarama as desired.
7. Use construction-paper scraps, scissors, and glue to create and add stand-up figures to the display.

Celebrate Memorial Day!

Read the paragraphs.

Memorial Day is a **patriotic holiday.** It is usually celebrated the last **Monday** in **May.** This holiday **honors** Americans who have died fighting for our country. Memorial Day is also called **Poppy** Day. Some people sell poppies (small red flowers) to help men and women who have fought in wars.

Memorial Day is celebrated in many ways. Some people place **flowers** and **flags** on the graves of honored men and women. Many towns have **parades.** Girl and Boy **Scouts** often march in the parades.

Solve the puzzle.
- Read the clues.
- Find the answers in the paragraphs. (Hint: They are in bold type!)
- Write the answers in the puzzle.

Bonus Box: Choose three words from the puzzle. On the back of this sheet, write a sentence with each of them.

Across:
1. a special day
5. describes a love for one's country
7. members of a group
8. patriotic symbols
9. a month

Down:
1. shows respect for
2. blossoms
3. events with marching bands
4. the day after Sunday
6. a small red flower

Name _____

Memorial Day Parade

Solve each problem.
Connect the answers in order from the least to the greatest to discover the parade route.

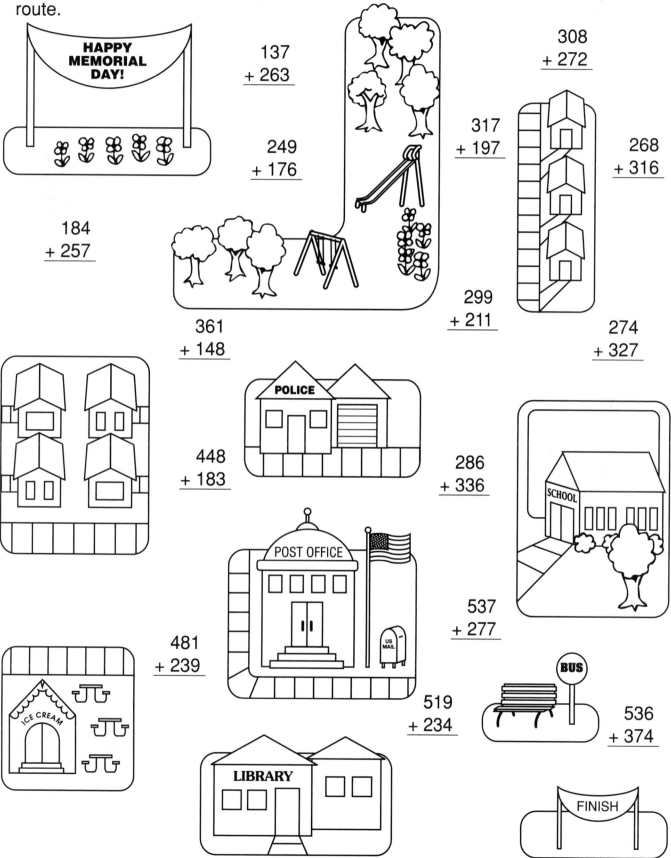

HAPPY MEMORIAL DAY!

137
+ 263

249
+ 176

308
+ 272

317
+ 197

268
+ 316

184
+ 257

299
+ 211

361
+ 148

274
+ 327

POLICE

448
+ 183

286
+ 336

SCHOOL

537
+ 277

481
+ 239

POST OFFICE
US MAIL

BUS

519
+ 234

536
+ 374

ICE CREAM

LIBRARY

FINISH

Name_____

A Salute To Subtraction

Solve each problem.
Color each flag that shows a correct answer.

1. 743 − 307 444 436	**2.** 317 − 189 128 228	**3.** 436 − 238 198 202
4. 653 − 472 185 181	**5.** 727 − 586 261 141	**6.** 915 − 345 570 750
7. 274 − 156 118 128	**8.** 538 − 247 371 291	**9.** 624 − 586 42 38
10. 952 − 270 722 682	**11.** 467 − 174 293 393	**12.** 836 − 627 209 211

Bonus Box: On the back of this sheet, use some of the remaining answers to write three subtraction problems. Ask a classmate to solve them.

National PHYSICAL FITNESS Month

Jump into these healthful activities to teach your students about the importance of being physically fit!

Physical Fitness Facts

The President's Council On Physical Fitness And Sports sponsors National Physical Fitness Month in May. This observance recognizes the importance of exercise. Regular exercise increases resistance to illness and strengthens muscles. When a person exercises, his muscles use up oxygen very quickly. To help oxygen get to his muscles, his heart beats faster. The number of times a heart pumps per minute is called the *pulse rate.* The more physically fit a person is, the quicker his pulse rate returns to normal after exercise.

Fitness Is "Fun-tastic"!

What better way to promote physical fitness than with a weekly exercise log. Tell youngsters that exercise not only helps people stay healthy; it can be a lot of fun, too! Have youngsters brainstorm types of physical activity—such as running, jumping rope, and bicycling—as you list their ideas on the chalkboard. Share with students the "Physical Fitness Facts" on this page. Then give each student a copy of page 40. Challenge each youngster to exercise every day for one week, and ask her to record her fitness activities on her sheet. At the end of the week, have each student illustrate and write about her favorite physical activity in the box beside her completed chart. Then ask her to circle the bear at the bottom of her page that corresponds with the number of times she exercised. If desired, present each student who exercised at least twice with a copy of a certificate on page 41.

Before And After

Give students *and* their math skills a workout! Explain to students that a *pulse* tells how fast a heart is beating. Tell youngsters that with this lesson they will discover how exercise affects pulse rate. Have each student take his pulse by placing an index finger on the wrist of his opposite hand and counting the beats in one minute. (A normal pulse rate for a youngster is 90 to 120 pulsations per minute.) Ask each student to write his number on a sheet of paper. Then, for approximately five minutes, engage students in a physical activity, such as jumping jacks or running in place. Have each youngster take his pulse again immediately after this activity and record it on his paper. Ask him to compare his pulse rates before and after exercising. What does he notice? If desired, repeat this activity on several other days and have each student record his pulse rates on a graph. Ask students to analyze their graphs and discuss their results.

Fitness Is "Fun-tastic"!

Follow your teacher's directions.

Day	Type Of Exercise	My Favorite Exercise This Week
Monday		
Tuesday		
Wednesday		
Thursday		
Friday		
Saturday		
Sunday		

It is important to exercise.
Circle the bear that shows how many times you exercised this week.

 0	1	2	3	4	5	6	7
Uh-oh! Try again next week.	**Not bad.** Try to exercise often.	**O.K.** Nice try!	**Good!** Keep it up!	**Great!** You worked hard!	**Wow!** What a workout!	**Super!** Way to go!	**Congratulations!** You're a fitness pro!

©1998 The Education Center, Inc. • *May Monthly Reproducibles* • Grades 2–3 • TEC953

Note To The Teacher: Use with "Fitness Is 'Fun-tastic'!" on page 39.

The key to good health is exercise!

_____
student

exercised _____ times this week!
number

Way to go!

_____   _____
teacher's signature   date

©1998 The Education Center, Inc. • _May Monthly Reproducibles_ • Grades 2–3 • TEC953

Wow!

_____
student

exercised _____ times this week!
number

Keep it up!

_____   _____
teacher's signature   date

©1998 The Education Center, Inc. • _May Monthly Reproducibles_ • Grades 2–3 • TEC953

Name _____

Exercise Your Mind!

Read and solve each problem.

1. Betsy Bear did 35 push-ups. Bo Bear did 43 push-ups. How many did they do in all?

R ____

2. In September, B. C. Bear could do 31 jumping jacks. In May he could do 58. How many more jumping jacks could he do in May?

E ____

3. Each day Betsy does 25 sit-ups. How many sit-ups does she do in four days?

X ____

4. Bert Bear played tennis for 10 minutes on Monday, 20 minutes on Tuesday, and 30 minutes on Wednesday. If he continues this pattern, how long will he play on Thursday?

S ____

5. B. C. ran around the track 14 times. Betsy ran around the track 17 times. How many times did they run around the track in all?

E ____

6. Bo and Barb Bear played basketball. Bo made 34 baskets. Barb made 18. How many more baskets did Bo make?

C ____

7. Bert can swim two laps in four minutes. At this rate, how many laps can he swim in eight minutes?

E ____

8. Barb can do 63 toe-touches. B. C. can do 59 toe-touches. How many toe-touches can they do in all?

I ____

Write each letter above the matching answer to complete the sentence.

Bear this in mind! It is important to __ __ __ __ __ __ __ __ __ .
4   100   31   78   16   122   40   27

42

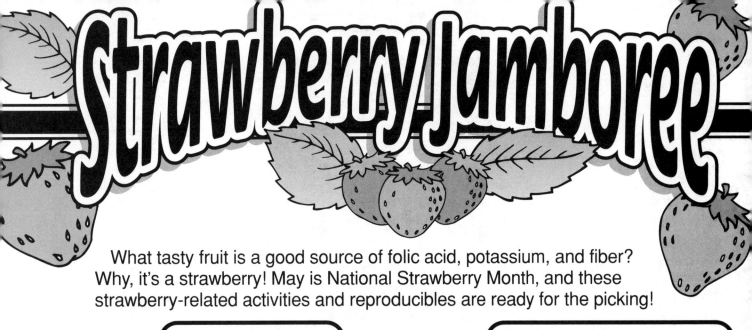

Strawberry Jamboree

What tasty fruit is a good source of folic acid, potassium, and fiber? Why, it's a strawberry! May is National Strawberry Month, and these strawberry-related activities and reproducibles are ready for the picking!

Tasty Topping
(Makes 2 pints)

Make and sample this recipe with students for a delicious introduction to " 'Strawberry-ific' Creations" on this page.

Ingredients:

4 cups hulled strawberries
4 cups sugar
1/4 teaspoon shredded lemon peel

3 ounces liquid fruit pectin
2 tablespoons lemon juice

Crush the berries; then mix in the sugar and lemon peel. Let the mixture stand for ten minutes. In a small bowl, combine the liquid pectin and the lemon juice. Add this mixture to the berries and stir for three minutes. Spoon the mixture into two pint containers, leaving a 1/2-inch headspace in each. Let the containers stand at room temperature for 24 hours. Then serve spoonfuls of the topping on foods such as ice cream, toast, or crackers. The remaining topping can be stored for three weeks in the refrigerator or up to one year in the freezer.

"Strawberry-ific" Creations

Promote creativity and teamwork with this mouthwatering activity! Give each student a sample of "Tasty Topping" (see recipe on this page) or another strawberry treat. Then divide students into small groups. Give each group two minutes to list on a sheet of paper as many foods that contain strawberries as they can. At the end of this time, have each group share its list. Next challenge each group to create a new recipe for strawberries, and ask them to record it on a recipe card–shaped paper. Then bind the completed recipes with a construction-paper cover to make a unique class cookbook. Yum!

The Poetry Patch

Inspire your young poets with this scrumptious topic! Ask students to brainstorm words that describe strawberries as you record their responses on the chalkboard. Then have each youngster use the brainstormed list to write a poem with the format shown.

Instruct each student to glue his completed poem onto a red construction-paper strawberry cutout. Next have him glue a construction-paper leaf and stem onto the strawberry. Then display the poems on a bulletin board titled "The Poetry Patch."

Line 1: Title (2 syllables)
Line 2: Description of title (4 syllables)
Line 3: Action (6 syllables)
Line 4: Feeling or statement (8 syllables)
Line 5: Repeated title or synonym (2 syllables)

Berries
Sweet and juicy
Picking some strawberries
Delicious with my cereal
Red fruit

44 Name _____

A "Berry" Special Card

Color the first strawberry.
Cut it out. Then cut it on the bold line to divide it in half.
Write a note on the second strawberry.
Cut it out.
Glue the colored strawberry pieces onto the shaded areas.

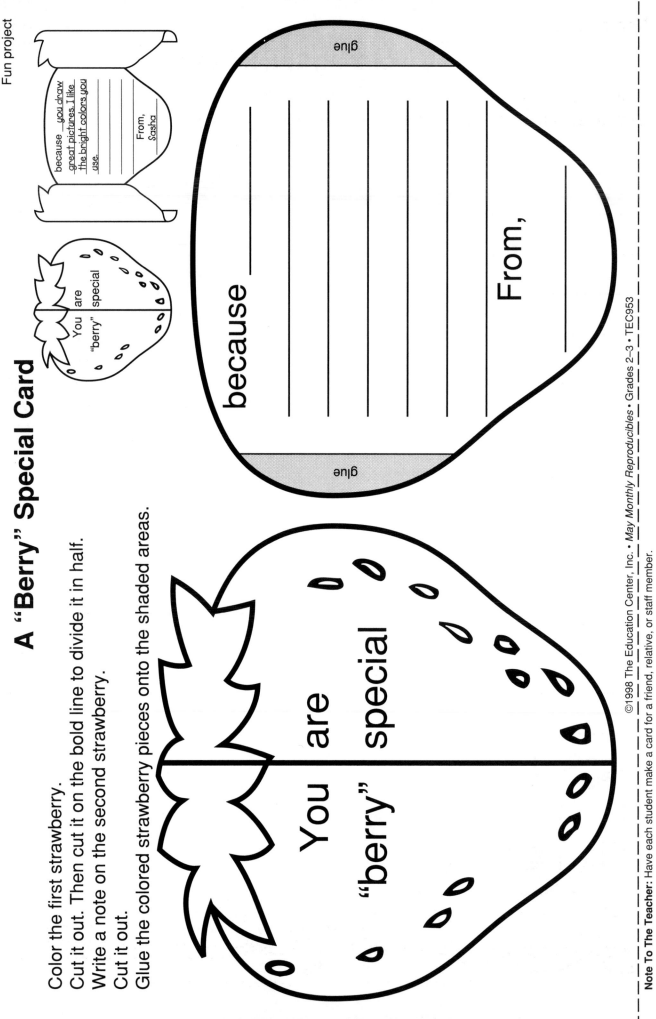

because _____

From, _____

You are "berry" special

because _you draw great pictures. I like the bright colors you use._

From,
Sasha

You are "berry" special

Note To The Teacher: Have each student make a card for a friend, relative, or staff member.

Appetizing Adjectives

Write about two of your favorite strawberry foods.
Use at least five adjectives from the Word Bank.

_____
_____
_____
_____
_____
_____
_____
_____

_____
_____
_____
_____
_____
_____

Word Bank

chewy	spicy
gooey	delicious
crunchy	sweet
smooth	sour
cold	tasty
hot	crispy
frozen	fresh
salty	creamy

Remember: An adjective is a describing word. It tells how something looks, feels, smells, tastes, or sounds.

Bonus Box: Think about your favorite place. On the back of this sheet, list at least five adjectives to describe it.

46

Just "Ripe" Math

Solve each problem.
If the answer matches the numeral on the leaf, color the berry red.

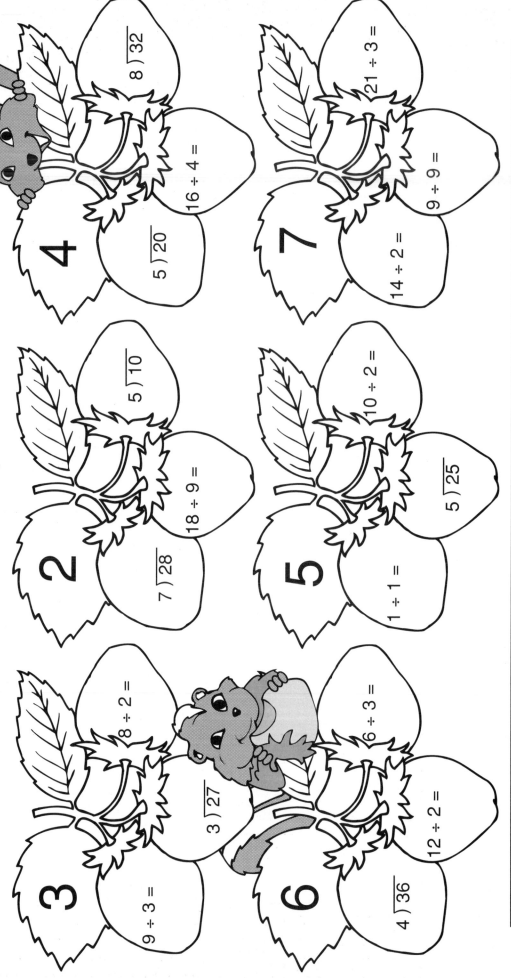

3
$9 \div 3 =$
$3\overline{)27}$
$8 \div 2 =$

2
$18 \div 9 =$
$7\overline{)28}$
$5\overline{)10}$

4
$16 \div 4 =$
$5\overline{)20}$
$8\overline{)32}$

6
$12 \div 2 =$
$4\overline{)36}$
$6 \div 3 =$

5
$1 \div 1 =$
$5\overline{)25}$
$10 \div 2 =$

7
$14 \div 2 =$
$9 \div 9 =$
$21 \div 3 =$

Bonus Box: There are 32 strawberries and 4 children. If they share the berries equally, how many would each child get? Show your work and solve the problem on the back of this sheet.

NATIONAL HAMBURGER MONTH

Serve up these mouthwatering activities in honor of National Hamburger Month! This tribute to burgers is sponsored by White Castle®, the original fast-food hamburger chain. Plain or with all the fixings, hamburgers have been an American favorite since the early 1920s.

Burger Bylines

Here's a writing activity that students will love to sink their teeth into! Give each student a copy of page 48 and several sheets of blank paper. Have each student cut out his hamburger pattern and place it atop the blank paper. Instruct him to staple the pattern and paper together at the top. Next have him firmly hold the stapled sheets and carefully cut the paper to the shape of the hamburger. Then tell students that on August 5, 1989, the world's largest hamburger was made at the Outgamie County Fairgrounds in Seymour, Wisconsin. It weighed 2 1/2 tons! Ask each student to write in his hamburger booklet a story about what he would do with a burger that large. Have him personalize his cover and pages as desired; then invite him to share his completed work. No doubt this tantalizing topic will result in some king-size appetites for writing!

Hold The Pickles!

Students will have a sizzling good time with this graphing activity! On a large sheet of bulletin-board or chart paper, draw a graph similar to the one shown. Then have each youngster write his name in the appropriate chart section to indicate his favorite hamburger condiment. Discuss the results with students; then have each youngster write three statements that describe the graph. Next ask students to predict how a graph of favorite hot dog condiments would compare to the completed hamburger graph. Design and complete a class graph of hot dog toppings in a like manner. Then compare results. How are the graphs alike? Different?

What do you like on your hamburger?					
16					
15					
14					
13					
12					
11					
10					
9	Beth				
8	Jake				
7	Emily				
6	Jean				
5	Alice	Jason			
4	Grace	Byron		Brooks	Jordan	Mike
3	Tom	Tim		Pam	Katie	Sue
2	John	Barbara	Kristie	Matt	Don	Melissa
1	Ann	Joe	Nancy	Tanner	Darcy	Bobby
	ketchup	mustard	relish	tomatoes	cheese	pickles

Order's Up!

It will be a race to the serving line with this fast-paced math game! Duplicate one copy of page 48. Draw a 10- or 12-space gameboard on the burger and add the labels "Place Your Order!" and "Order's Up!" as shown. Then duplicate the gameboard and page 49 on construction paper for each student. Have each student personalize and cut out her game cards (a resealable plastic bag can be used for easy storage). To play this partner or small-group game, each player shuffles her cards and stacks them facedown on a playing surface. Then she places a game piece, such as a kidney bean or penny, at the starting line on her gameboard. In turn, each player draws a card from her deck and solves the math problem. If the answer is correct, as determined by the other player(s), she moves forward one space on her gameboard. An incorrect answer does not earn a space. If a player draws a phrase card, she moves her game piece as indicated on the card. Play continues in a like manner until one player has reached the finish line. She then calls, "Order's Up!" and is declared the winner.

Pattern

Use with "Order's Up!" and "Burger Bylines" on page 47.

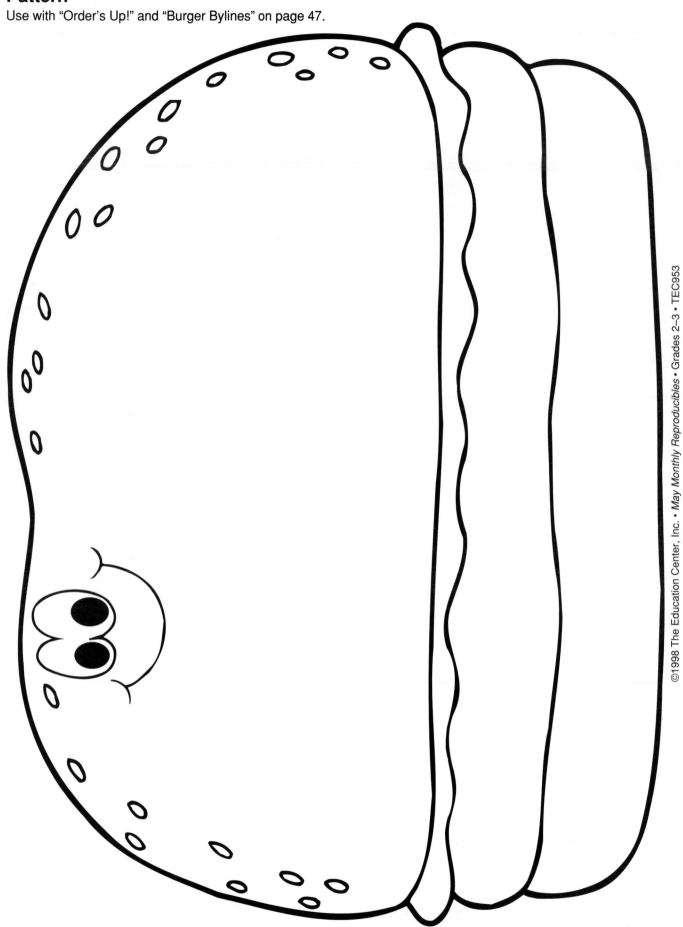

5 x 5	7 x 3	6 x 4	8 x 6
9 x 6	5 x 3	7 x 8	9 x 3
6 x 6	8 x 4	5 x 9	7 x 7
8 x 8	5 x 4	9 x 8	9 x 9
Your burger burned! Lose a turn.	Buy two burgers for the price of one! Move ahead two spaces.	There is a waiting line. Lose a turn.	You add fries to your order. Move ahead two spaces.

Lunch At The Burger Palace

Read each problem.
Write a matching fraction
  beside each picture.
Two have been done for you.

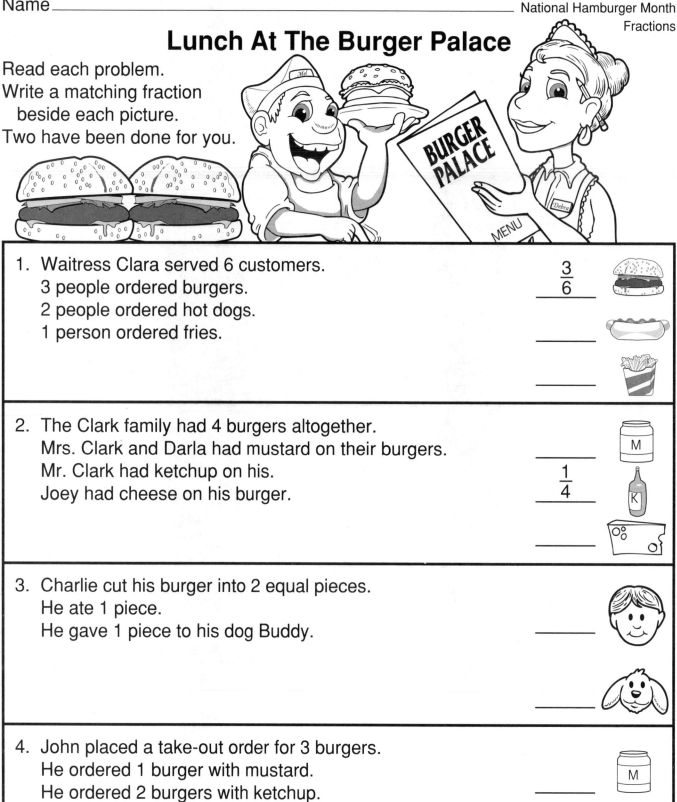

1. Waitress Clara served 6 customers.
   3 people ordered burgers.
   2 people ordered hot dogs.
   1 person ordered fries.

   $\frac{3}{6}$

   _____

   _____

2. The Clark family had 4 burgers altogether.
   Mrs. Clark and Darla had mustard on their burgers.
   Mr. Clark had ketchup on his.
   Joey had cheese on his burger.

   _____

   $\frac{1}{4}$

   _____

3. Charlie cut his burger into 2 equal pieces.
   He ate 1 piece.
   He gave 1 piece to his dog Buddy.

   _____

   _____

4. John placed a take-out order for 3 burgers.
   He ordered 1 burger with mustard.
   He ordered 2 burgers with ketchup.

   _____

   _____

Bonus Box: Draw and color a restaurant picture on the back of this sheet. Below the picture, write at least one fraction that tells about the picture.

Mother's Day

The celebration of Mother's Day in the United States began many years ago. Julia Ward Howe made the first known suggestion for a day honoring mothers in 1872. Thirty-five years later, Anna Jarvis began a campaign for a nationwide observance of Mother's Day. She also started the tradition of wearing a carnation on this day. Jarvis worked hard to gain support for her cause, and in 1915, President Woodrow Wilson signed a proclamation that declared the second Sunday in May Mother's Day.

*M*akes the world's best cookies
*O*ften tells great jokes
*M*eans a lot to me

by _____ Tim _____

Heartfelt Poetry

These poetic gifts from the heart are sure to please! Have students brainstorm words that begin with the letter *m;* then list the words on the chalkboard. Brainstorm and record words that begin with the letter *o* in a similar manner. Next give each student a copy of page 52. Ask each youngster to use the letters in the word "mom" to write an acrostic about his mother. Encourage students to refer to the brainstormed lists as they work. Have each student color and personalize his heart as desired, being careful to leave the words clearly visible. Then ask him to cut out his heart and present his completed poem to his mother.

Coupons For Mom

Here's a priceless gift-book idea for Mother's Day! Discuss with students small jobs or favors they can do to help their mothers. Then give each student a copy of page 53. Have each student write in the small blank box a helpful deed that she would like to do for her mother, then add an illustration in the box beside it. Ask her to color and personalize all of the boxes as desired, then cut them out. Instruct each youngster to stack the resulting pages in sequential order, place the cover atop them, and staple the entire stack on the left edge. To use a coupon, the student's mother cuts off the corresponding phrase and presents it to her youngster. There's no doubt mothers will love cashing in these handy coupons!

Recommended Literature

Read with students these books about marvelous moms and their families!

The Mother's Day Mice by Eve Bunting (Clarion Books, 1988)
George Washington's Mother by Jean Fritz (Grosset & Dunlap, Inc.; 1992)
We're Very Good Friends, My Mother And I by P. K. Hallinan (Ideals Children's Books, 1990)
Mama Is A Miner by George Ella Lyon (Orchard Books, 1994)
Love You Forever by Robert Munsch (Firefly Books Ltd., 1986)

Pattern

Use with "Heartfelt Poetry"
on page 51.

$\mathcal{M}$
o
$\mathcal{M}$

by _____

1

help with
the laundry

3

5

When it's a helping hand that
you need,
Just clip a coupon for the deed.

help with dinner

a job of your choice

2

4

Coupons For Mom

From _____

©1998 The Education Center, Inc.

Name_____

Mother's Day Math

Mr. Smith's class made Mother's
Day presents.
The graph shows how many
students made each type
of gift.

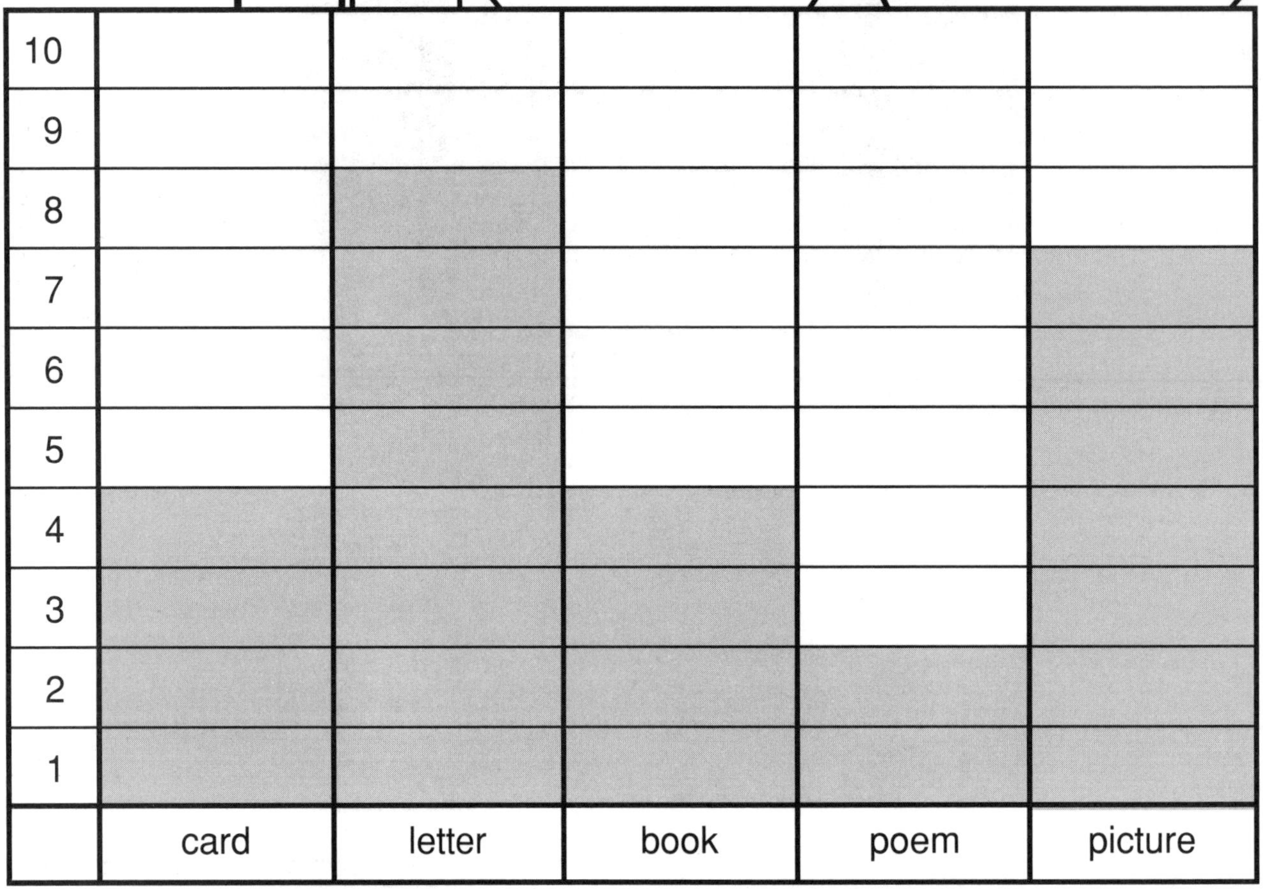

	card	letter	book	poem	picture
10					
9					
8		▨			
7		▨			▨
6		▨			▨
5		▨			▨
4	▨	▨	▨		▨
3	▨	▨	▨		▨
2	▨	▨	▨	▨	▨
1	▨	▨	▨	▨	▨

Read the graph.
Answer the questions.

1. What gift was made by the most students? _____

2. What gift was made by the fewest students? _____

3. How many more letters than pictures were made?_____

4. How many more pictures were made than books *and* poems? _____

5. How many more poems are needed to equal the number of cards *and* letters?

_____

6. How many students made gifts? _____

Bonus Box: Choose one of the items on the graph. Make it for a Mother's Day gift!

National WEATHER OBSERVER'S Day

Weather followers everywhere can enjoy National Weather Observer's Day on May 4. "Weather" or not the day's forecast is appealing, your classroom is sure to be brighter with these sunny activities and reproducibles.

Who Needs To Know?

Who needs to listen to the weather forecast each day? A better question is, Who *doesn't?* With this simple writing activity, students will quickly realize that the weather affects almost everyone. Ask youngsters to brainstorm careers, and record their responses on the chalkboard. Have students identify how the people who do each job may be affected by the weather; then ask each youngster to select a career from the brainstormed list. Next instruct her to write the following sentence at the bottom of a sheet of drawing paper: "The weather is important to a(n) _____ because _____." Then have her complete the sentence based on her chosen career. Finally, ask each student to illustrate her sentence. Bind the completed pages with a construction-paper cover and add the title "Who Says The Weather Is Important?"

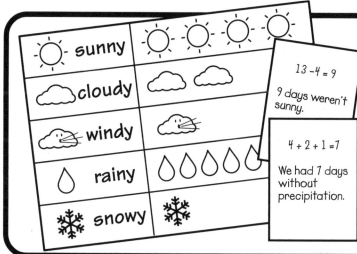

Daily Data

It's a breeze to make and use this weather-tracking pictograph! On a large sheet of bulletin-board paper, prepare a chart like the one shown. Each morning ask a different student to draw in the appropriate space the symbol that corresponds with the day's weather. Periodically review the data with students, and have each youngster write a number sentence to represent some of the graph's information. Then ask her to write a sentence explaining her work. Now that's a "sun-sational" way to record the weather *and* reinforce math skills!

The Weather Is Shaping Up

This poetry-writing activity will cause a flurry of excitement among your students. Have each youngster draw a simple weather-related picture, such as the sun, a cloud, a raindrop, or a lightning bolt. Then encourage each young poet to think of words that define or describe the pictured item. Have him list the words around the outline of his picture to create a shape poem. Give students an opportunity to share their completed poems; then display them on a brightly colored bulletin board. Students will love this poetry form, and that's a forecast you can count on!

Weather Watch

Write the month and dates on the calendar.
Use the key to record each day's weather.

Sunday	Monday	Tuesday	Wednesday	Thursday	Friday	Saturday

Key

☀ sunny   ☁ cloudy

💧 rainy   🌬 windy

❄ snowy

At the end of the month, count the symbols.

How many days were sunny? _____

cloudy? _____   rainy? _____

windy? _____   snowy? _____

Bonus Box: On the back of this sheet, write three sentences about the information you collected.

Where Are The Weather Words?

Read the page numbers and words on the umbrella.
On each raindrop, write the page number for the entry word.

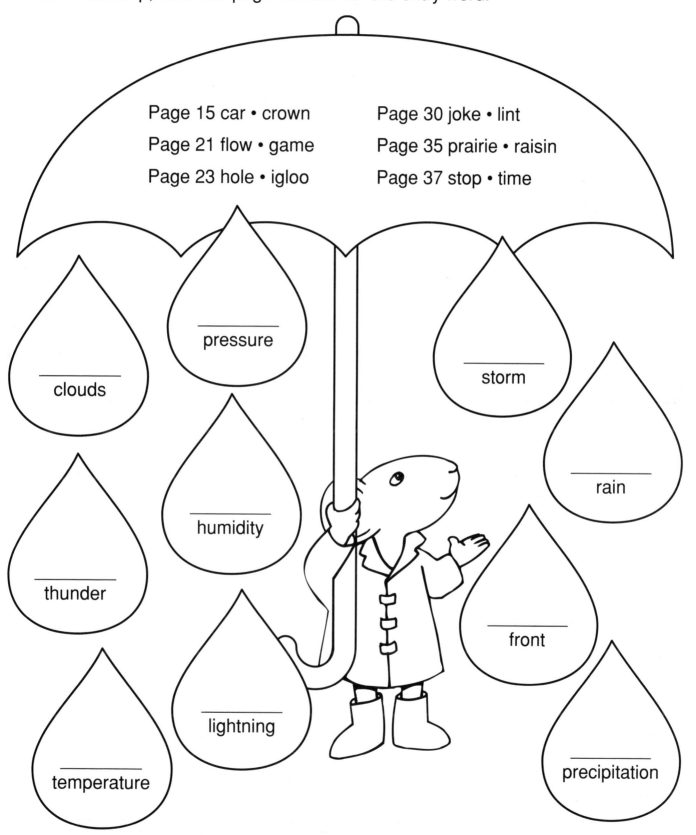

Page 15 car • crown
Page 21 flow • game
Page 23 hole • igloo

Page 30 joke • lint
Page 35 prairie • raisin
Page 37 stop • time

pressure

clouds

storm

rain

thunder

humidity

front

temperature

lightning

precipitation

Tracking The Weather

A **front** is a boundary between warm and cold air masses.
Fronts can move, bringing cold air and storms, or warm air and gentle rain.
On a map, the ▲ and ◖ front symbols point in the direction that the front is moving.

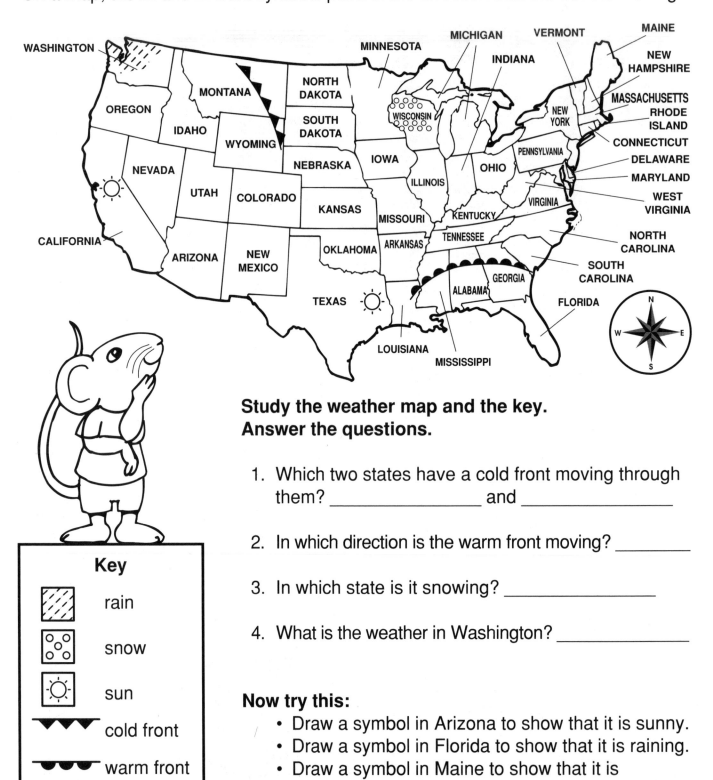

Study the weather map and the key.
Answer the questions.

1. Which two states have a cold front moving through
   them? _____ and _____

2. In which direction is the warm front moving? _____

3. In which state is it snowing? _____

4. What is the weather in Washington? _____

Now try this:
- Draw a symbol in Arizona to show that it is sunny.
- Draw a symbol in Florida to show that it is raining.
- Draw a symbol in Maine to show that it is snowing.

Key

▨	rain
⊡	snow
☼	sun
▼▼▼	cold front
●●●	warm front

SPLASH INTO SUMMER!

It's time to say "Good-bye" to school and "Hello" to summer. So dive right into these fun-filled year-end activities!

Once Written, Twice Shared

Send off one class of students *and* welcome another with one simple project! Give each student a lined 5" x 7" index card and ask her to illustrate the unlined side with her favorite activity of the school year. Then instruct her to visually divide the lined side in the middle. Have each student write a description of her picture and sign her name on the left side, and then write this address on the right side: New [grade] Grader, [teacher's name]'s Class, [school name]. Revisit lots of fun times by having each student share her postcard. At the beginning of the next school year, give each of your new students one of the completed postcards to build anticipation for the year ahead!

We went on a field trip to the museum. We saw lots of neat things. Bethany

New 2nd Grader Mrs. M.'s Class Truman School

Year-End Raffle

Provide an incentive for good student behavior and prepare your classroom for summer at the same time! During the last month of school, when a student demonstrates positive behavior, present him with a "ticket" (small construction-paper square or strip). At the end of each day, have him write his name on each of his tickets and place them in a designated container. For a raffle prize, select a poster, game, or a class book or project that you will not need or want for the following school year. Then draw a ticket from the jar and present the winning student with the prize. Repeat this process for a desired number of days. In no time at all, your classroom will be clutter-free!

A Poetic Send-Off

Here's a picture-perfect student gift! Snap a class photo of your students; then photocopy a class set or have a class supply of prints made. For each student, label the front of a construction-paper folder with his name. Attach a photo (or copy) to the inside of the folder with photo mounts or tape. Next glue a copy of the poem shown opposite the photo and sign your name. Present each student with this special class memento on the last day of school.

A Special Good-bye

This shell-shaped booklet will ease your youngsters from the last days of school into the first days of summer! For each student, duplicate pages 61–62. Also give each student one copy of a cover on page 60; then ask him to cut out the cover and booklet pages. Next instruct each student to stack his pages in sequential order, place the cover atop them, and staple the entire stack where indicated. Have each youngster personalize his cover as desired and complete pages 1 and 2 independently. Then provide an opportunity for students to share their work with classmates. Next have each student collect his classmates' autographs on page 3. Finally, before students take their booklets home, encourage them to read lots of books during the summer and record them on page 4 as indicated.

Teaching you has been a treat.
The fun we've had just can't be beat.
Although it's time to say, "So long,"
This picture will keep class memories strong.

Mrs. Clark

Booklet Covers
Use with "A Special Good-bye" on page 59.

Splash
Into
Summer!

_____

Name

©1998 The Education Center, Inc. • *May Monthly Reproducibles* • *Grades 2–3* • *TEC953*

Splash
Into
Summer!

_____

Name

©1998 The Education Center, Inc. • *May Monthly Reproducibles* • *Grades 2–3* • *TEC953*

Hold On To The Good Times!

Draw a special memory of this school year in each box.

1

Going Places

Draw a blue wave under each place that you might visit this summer.
- the mall
- the movies
- a park
- a pool
- a relative's house
- a friend's house
- another state
- another country

If you could go anywhere, where would you go?

_____
_____

2

Leave Your Mark!

Collect your friends' autographs.

3

A Reading Collection

Be "shore" to read lots of books this summer. Color a seashell for each kind of book you read.

mystery

animal story

biography

humorous story

4

jokes or riddles

fairy tale

nonfiction

Answer Keys

Page 8
1. victory
2. French
3. fireworks
4. Mexico
5. May
6. fiesta
7. freedom

Page 9
1. Tortillas
2. Cinco De Mayo
3. piñata
4. mariachi
5. Iguana
6. sombrero
7. flor

Page 10
1. 494 (red)
2. 676 (green)
3. 879 (green)
4. 822 (green)
5. 361 (red)
6. 561 (green)
7. 411 (red)
8. 586 (green)
9. 688 (green)
10. 205 (red)
11. 497 (red)
12. 712 (green)

Bonus Box:
205, 361, 411, 494, 497

Page 15
1. float
2. fly
3. friend
4. frog
5. grass
6. green
7. leap
8. leg
9. splash
10. spot
11. tadpole
12. tail

Page 16
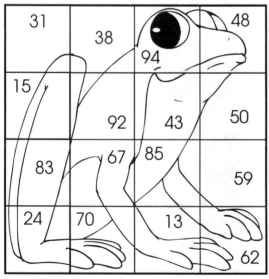

Page 20
1. Answers will vary.
2. Busy
3. Sting
4. Buzz and Zip
5. Answers will vary.
6. Answers will vary.

Page 21
1. they make their homes in wood or under bark.
2. they sometimes build homes in tunnels made by other bees.
3. she wants to protect her young.
4. they dig holes in wooden porches and barns.
5. they want to cool their hive.

Bonus Box: carpenter bees, honeybees, leaf-cutting bees, mason bees, mining bees

Page 22
1. week
2. deer
3. sea
4. tale
5. board
6. right
7. new
8. bare
9. plain
10. pear
11. son
12. maid

Page 26
Step 1: Cook the ground beef and onions together.
Step 2: After the meat and onions are cooked, drain the fat.
Step 3: Add the rest of the ingredients to the cooked meat and onions.
Step 4: Stir all of the ingredients together; then cook the mixture for one hour.
Step 5: Serve the chili to a heap of hungry cowboys.

Page 28
1. 73
2. 49
3. 70
4. 18
5. 16
6. 31
7. 5
8. 6
9. 51
10. 42

Page 33
The order of answers may vary.

find / discover
bucket / pail
fast / quick
little / small
jump / leap
keep / save
alike / same
cool / chilly
ocean / sea

Answer Keys

Page 36

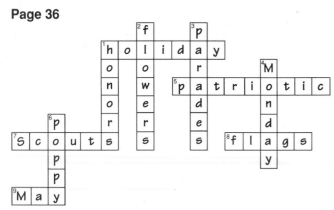

Crossword:
- 1 across: holiday
- 2 down: flowers
- 3 down: parades
- 4 down: Monday
- 5 across: patriotic
- 6 down: poppy
- 7 across: Scouts
- 8 across: flags
- 9 across: May
- honor

Page 37

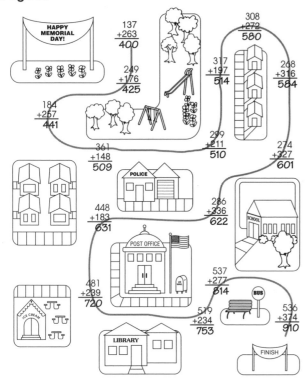

HAPPY MEMORIAL DAY!

137 + 263 = 400
249 + 176 = 425
184 + 257 = 441
361 + 148 = 509
448 + 183 = 631
481 + 239 = 720
308 + 272 = 580
317 + 197 = 514
268 + 316 = 584
299 + 211 = 510
274 + 327 = 601
286 + 336 = 622
537 + 277 = 814
519 + 234 = 753
536 + 374 = 910

POLICE · SCHOOL · POST OFFICE · LIBRARY · ICE CREAM · BUS · FINISH

Page 38

1. 436	5. 141	9. 38
2. 128	6. 570	10. 682
3. 198	7. 118	11. 293
4. 181	8. 291	12. 209

Page 42

1. 78	5. 31
2. 27	6. 16
3. 100	7. 4
4. 40	8. 122

EXERCISE

Page 46

3: $8 \div 2 = 4$ · $7\overline{)28}$ · $9 \div 3 = 3$ · $3\overline{)27} = 9$ · $18 \div 9 = 2$
2: $5\overline{)10} = 2$
4: $8\overline{)32} = 4$ · $5\overline{)20} = 4$ · $16 \div 4 = 4$
6: $6 \div 3 = 2$ · $4\overline{)36} = 9$ · $12 \div 2 = 6$
5: $1 + 1 = 1$ · $10 \div 2 = 5$ · $5\overline{)25} = 5$
7: $14 \div 2 = 7$ · $21 \div 3 = 7$ · $9 \div 9 = 1$

Bonus Box: $32 \div 4 = 8$ berries for each child (Problem-solving method will vary.)

Page 50

1. 2/6 hot dogs
   1/6 fries
2. 2/4 mustard
   1/4 cheese
3. 1/2 Charlie
   1/2 Buddy
4. 1/3 mustard
   2/3 ketchup

Page 54

1. letter
2. poem
3. one
4. one
5. ten
6. 25

Page 57

pressure 35
clouds 15
humidity 23
thunder 37
lightning 30
temperature 37
storm 37
rain 35
front 21
precipitation 35

Page 58

1. Montana
   Wyoming
2. north
3. Wisconsin
4. rain